Bloodfire

Also by Fred Chappell

The World Between the Eyes

It Is Time, Lord

The Inkling

Dagon

The Gaudy Place

River

LOUISIANA STATE UNIVERSITY PRESS

Bloodfire A Poem

Fred Chappell

BATON ROUGE AND LONDON   1978

Copyright © 1978 by Fred Chappell
All rights reserved
Manufactured in the United States of America
Designer: Albert Crochet
Type Face: VIP Garamond
Typesetter: New Hampshire Composition, Concord, N.H.
Printer:Thomson-Shore, Inc.
Binder: John H. Dekker & Sons, Inc.

Parts of this poem have previously appeared in these magazines:
Archive, Guilford Review, Little Review, Small Farm, and *Vanderbilt
Poetry Review;* and in the anthology *Mountain Paths.*

LIBRARY OF CONGRESS CATALOGING IN PUBLICATION DATA

Chappell, Fred, 1936-
  Bloodfire.

  CONTENTS: Fire now wakening on the river.—Rimbaud
fire letter to Jim Applewhite.—My father allergic to
fire.—Feverscape, the silver planet. [etc.]
  I. Title.
PS3553.H298B57   811'.5'4   78-13578
ISBN 0-8071-0451-5
ISBN 0-8071-0452-3 pbk.

Dedicated to
Frank & Grace DiSanto
and to
Robert & Nancy Morgan
and to the memory of
Mrs. Rebecca Chappell

This is the hour when windows escape houses to catch fire at the end of the world where our world is going to dawn.

René Char

Contents

Bloodfire

I   Fire Now Wakening on the River

Morning.
First light shapes the trees.

  Behind tensed lids begins the salvo
Of silent orange curtain, little by little rising, changing
In rising to the sky-wide hem of the northern *Borealis*.
In alert half-sleep I follow upward the supernal sheer
Of burning drapery.
    Between lid and pupil
The façade of first-light comes floating.
Air-galleons of touchless fire drift above the whitened river.

How, love, in this frenzy of illuminant particles, each atom a spark,
May I you touch?
   My forehead enters your shoulder
As air and flame enjoin, nothing separate,
All selfless in all as we burn together,
Ascend the air we make, wavering, visible.
We waver within one another.
The world in sunlit half-sleep is a film of fire.

It is a forest of fire suspended; the animals
That live in fire—that burning tiger, firefly and salamander, firedrake—
Observe us with their slash eyes,
See us rise in air as they rise in air,
See us twine as above a candle the yellow and red entwine.
Our bloods ascend this stalk of air like the snakes of a caduceus.
At last in fire we two are one and none.

The limits consume themselves, it is an ecstasy
Of forgetting and aspiring, how can this tight bedroom
Contain us?

(Our half-sleep of whitened waters
Rises, the river thrusts sunward
Its refracted columns. Cloud-margins the color of lit fuses.)

Or wind diving out of the sky and driving the flames forward,
Small flames like dog teeth
Biting the black circle larger, larger;
Green growth curls surly on the widening circle,
Boiled juices of poison oak smear the air a greasy window.
                This wilderness of doubt
We clear for our rough hovel, root the stump up
To lay our smooth hearthstone.

                            Now shall I clutch your life
In the fitful bed. Born troublous, elusive
As the spark flown upward, you shall not now escape
My net of furious dream.

I dream your mouth gasps open unbreathing,
Your arms outstretched above your head, swimmer
Of the heated air, you launch to sound the divided deeps of void.
                This way the world was formed,
The purer spirits surged ever upward,
Shucking the gross pig-matter their bodies;
Lie glittering round the zenith like strewn glass.
Mountain and riverbed are the stacked dead husks.
The pure spirits stand among monsters and heroes,
Orion, Hercules, Cassiopeia,
And Draco and the Big and Little Bear.
And we this hour, 28 May 1971,
Are Gemini:
          the Twins, each each and the other
Like the two-colored candleflame.

Torn sheet of light sizzles in the mirror:

The seeds, ignis semina, of fire
Put forth in me their rootlets, the tree of fire
Begins to shape itself.

I have no wish to awake,
Ever to awake, to be exiled a cinder
From my globe of half-dream,
To be born stark ignorant in my thirty-fifth year.

Trees fully aglow,
I reach for clothing.

To be fresh born at thirty-five,
That is a death.
          My flesh unburns
In coolness of morning.

II   Rimbaud Fire Letter to Jim Applewhite

That decade with Rimbaud I don't regret.
But could not live again. Man, that was *hard.*
Nursing the artificial fevers, wet
With Falstaff beer, I walked the railyard,
Stumbled the moon-streaked tracks, reciting line
After burning line I couldn't understand.
In the long twilight I waited for a sign
The world its symbols would mount at my command.

My folks thought I was crazy, maybe I was.
Drinking behind the garbage back of Maxine's Grill,
I formulated esoteric laws
That nothing ever obeyed, or ever will.
"Les brasiers, pleuvant aux rafales de givre.—Douceurs!"
I must have dreamed those words a hundred times,
But what they meant, or even what they *were,*
I never knew. They glowed in my head like flames.

Four things I knew: Rimbaud was genius pure;
The colors of the vowels and verb tenses;
That civilization was going up in fire;
And how to derange every last one of my senses:
Kind of a handbook on how to be weird and silly.
It might have helped if I had known some French,
But like any other Haywood County hillbilly
The simple thought of the language made me flinch.

So passed my high school years. The senior prom
I missed, and the girls, and all the thrilling sports.
My teachers asked me, "Boy, where you *from?*"
"From deep in a savage forest of unknown words."
The dialogue went downhill after that,

4

But our positions were clear respectively:
They stood up for health and truth and light,
I stood up for Baudelaire and me.

The subject gets more and more embarrassing.
Should I mention the clumsy shrine I built
In the maple tree behind old Plemmons' spring?
Or how I played the young Artur to the hilt
In beer joints where the acrid farmers drank?
Or how I tried to make my eyes look *through?*
—I'd better not. Enough, that I stayed drunk
For eight hot years, and came up black and blue.

One trouble was that time was running out.
Rimbaud had finished "all that shit" before
He reached his nineteenth year. I had about
Nineteen short months to get down to the core.
I never did, of course. I wrote a bunch
Of junk I'm grateful to have burned; I read
Some books. But my courage was totally out to lunch.
Oh, Fred Fred Fred Fred Fred . . .

Remember when we met our freshman year?
Not something you'd want to repeat, I guess, for still
R. worked his will in me, a blue blear
Smoke poured forth. (That, and alcohol.)
(And an army of cranky opinions about whatever
Topic was brought up.) (And a hateful pose
Of expertise.) Jesus, was I clever!
And smelt myself as smelling like a rose.

I had a wish, "Mourir aux fleuves barbares,"
And to fulfill it could have stayed at home.
But down at Duke in 1954
(*I like Ike*) it carried weight with some
Few wild men and true who wanted to write
And even tried to write—God bless them
Everyone!—and who scheduled the night
For BEER and the explication of a POEM.

Well, you recall: Mayola's Chili House,
Annamaria's Pizza, Maitland's Top Hat,
The Pickwick, and that truly squalid place,
The Duchess, where the local whores stayed fat
On college boys, and the Blue Star, the I.
P.D. But the joint that really made us flip
Sat sunsoaked on Broad St., where we walked by
Rambeau's Barber Shop.

Those were the days! . . . —But they went on and on and on.
The failure I saw myself grew darker and darker.
And hearing the hard new myths from Bob Mirandon,
I got Rimbaud confused with Charlie Parker.
It was a mess, mon vieux. Finally
They kicked me out, and back to the hills I went.
But not before they'd taught me how to see
Myself as halfway halved and halfway blent.

Jim, we talked our heads off. What didn't we say?
We didn't say what it cost our women to prop
Our psyches up, we couldn't admit *the day*
And age belonged still to our fathers. One drop
Distillate of Carolina reality
Might have cured much, but they couldn't make us drink.
We kept on terribly seeing how to see,
We kept on terribly thinking how to think.

They turned me down for the army. I wanted it raw,
I wanted to find a wound my mother could love.
("Il a deux trous rouges au côté droit.")
I wanted Uncle Sugar to call my bluff . . .
No soap. I wound up hauling fertilizer,
Collecting bills, and trying to read Rimbaud
At night, and preaching those poems to David Deas or
Anyone else I thought might care to know.

The only good thing was that I got married.
And I watched the mountains until the mountains touched

My mind and partly tore away my fire-red
Vision of a universe besmirched.
I started my Concordance to Samuel Johnson,
And learned to list a proper footnote, got down
To reading folks like Pope and Bertrand Bronson,
And turned my back on the ashes of Paree-town.

But as my father said, "Fire's in the bloodstream."
The groaning it cost my muse to take off my edge
Still sounds in my sleep, rasps my furious dream.
—Tell you what, Jim: let's grow old and sage;
Let's don't wind up brilliant, young, and dead.
Let's just remember.
                                        —Give my love to Jan.
Yours for terror and symbolism,
                                                    ole Fred.

28 May 1971

III   My Father Allergic to Fire

My father said: "The South is in love with fire.
You're eighteen, you're old enough to witness.
Barn-burnings, house-burnings, field-burnings . . . Anything
You want to name, we'll put to kerosene.
I can't say why. Maybe we caught it from Sherman."
On Hogback Ridge he kicked the cookstove, muttering.
The cabin whimpered at the corners, December
Predawn wind ripping down off the toothy
Rock-knob mountain top.
                              "What's the matter
With the stove?" I asked.
                              "Nothing, except you've got
To show this bitch who's boss. These old wood ranges,
They ought to keep half-hot. We don't come up
Hunting often enough so this one's accustomed.
Give her a kick if you want to hear her rumble.

"Anyhow, the South and fire: in the bloodstream,
Boy. The preachers preach it; it's all they know,
How we'll fry like bacon in the afterlife.
Maybe hellfire is good for the South, a kind
Of purgative. We could use a lot of that."

"What you talking?"
                       He grinned; and broke two eggs
Into a panful of grease. "One kind of fire, though,
Will make me ill to the vomiting point. My belly
When they burn those crosses comes up into my mouth."

Eighteen years of gingerly middle-class
Bringing-up prevented me. Newspaper
Accounts were all I knew, and ever would.
"The world," I told my dad, "is full of bastards.

Choosing the Klan to get dog-sick about,
That's like choosing a particular beggar's-lice."

"Because I joined the Klan." His voice was quiet
And dark and empty as an abandoned well.

"You joined the *what?*" (Trying not to giggle.)

"It's true, though. Not that I offered harm to black folks
Or dressed up in percales . . .   I was nine,
And messing around behind the packhouse, the way
A kid will mess around. Here came my brother
And a fellow I'd never seen. What made me duck
Underneath the packhouse and sit in the soft cool dust
With my chin propped on my knees I couldn't tell you.
I wasn't spying on my brother, anyhow
Not really spying—maybe like Leatherstocking.
(I'd read a fair-sized pile of Fenimore Cooper.)
I sat fiddling my fingers in the dust, breathing
The cool, and heard—nothing. Not one word.
Just a blurry clutter of older voices.
And all I could see were pairs of cut-off legs.
That got plenty boring. When I crawled out
They grabbed me, started asking what I heard.
Nothing, I kept saying, but they were scared."

"Of what?" I asked.
                    "Of themselves," he said. "What else?
They were kids like me playing in the dust.
They might have been pirates or cowboys if they hadn't caught
The germ. But they'd talked themselves into the Klan,
And they were taking it serious as death.
You would too, given the time and place . . .
So I had to be initiated. They
Thought that would make them safe, me being one
Of them, whatever it was they thought they were."

"Initiated how?"
                    He turned and sat down

At the table. "They said some mumbly-jumbly I didn't
Understand, and gouged some blood from my thumb,
And burned the cross on me."
                              "'Burned what?"
                                            "The cross."
He undid his shirt halfway. "Took kitchen matches
And heated the flat of the pocket knife blade
And branded my hide. Look here." Peeled back two layers
Of undershirt and bared his shoulder to me.
"It hurt like fury. They didn't like it either,
But this was the pinch they'd conspired themselves into."

"I don't see anything."
                        "It's forty years.
Look close."
              I stared into my father's skin.
A little pimple in a square of gray-pink flesh.
I peered as into a fog that held my future,
And no cross glowed there silver, no cross at all.
"Can't you see it?" He pleaded like a child.

My father's innocent shoulder I almost kissed.

"Can't you—?"
                "I see it now," I said. "It's smaller
Than I thought it'd be. It's really awfully small."

He breathed in deep relief and buttoned his shirt.
"Maybe now it is, but there was a time
It felt as big as the moon."
                              "That time is past."

"No time is past they made you shed blood on."

"The time for frying eggs is past," I said.
He opened his eyes. The cabin was full of smoke.

IV   Feverscape: The Silver Planet

Tensed lids or open eyes. Landscape the color of Jesus-words
in the testament, or color of sun on the gold-red edge.
Umber fire in my head the books and fevers drove me upon.

No illness passed me by; I lay in the sheets and boiled.
Firetree of illness spread over me,
I saw red sky through stained-glass leaves.

In the red wall of illness I saw Blackbeard
with his face afire, Dimaggio's bat like a flamethrower;
and the soldiers and cities went red as maple leaves.

I swallowed the Second World War off the greasy *Lifes'*,
photos of Hitler and the cordwood dead, waiting for Dr. Payne
to beckon me in to his chisel and meat saw.

Always above me the bronze angels of sickness hovered
like church bells, faces hidden, hands hidden.
The sheet was a snow of fire. I saw fever take on flesh.

My visitor most frequent was the Planet of Silver Fire.
Size of a basketball between bed and ceiling. Its color
was the color of beveled glass. The rainbow of fear.

Planet within whose continents I saw libraries
of Holy Bibles melt to gas, continents of ash-scab like
griffons and fern-faced witches thirsting for my marrow.

The oceans of the Silver Planet glowed with the horrible fishes
in the encyclopedia: Dragonfish, Sea Viper, Lamprotoxu,
Chiasmodon, like threads of tungsten in light bulbs.

And at its poles the shiniest fires: vast leaping
coronas fingered the medicine space I suffered in,
scrawled prescriptions on the tipped ceiling.

White tentacles of camphor-smelling flame the Silver
Planet lashed me with, each wound an alien word,
arms of fire scribbling me in the steamy bed.

I died of all those illnesses I didn't die of.
Whole duchies of my spirit went to inhabit
the stainless fires of the Silver Planet.

So I know well what sickness comes trembling over
the edge of the world. It is the great and
gleaming wolf spider with cunning caution.

And have become your stranger tarrying here,
your special leper.
Taste me to taste somewhat that Planet.

Yet still we must believe somewhere
exists the true cool dark forbidden us.
We want to wash our faces in it.

Too long we have bared our backs, we
have bent our heads beneath the cruel silver fire.
The nerves keep smoldering but never catch.

V   Firewood

Flame flame where I hit now, the cat is scared, heart
red in the oak where sun
climbed vein by vein to seek the cool
wedge hard where I strike now and rose
leaves drop off as if ruin of cloud on cloud
fell, heart of red oak strips to sunlight,
sunlight chopped like this to pie chunks,
like this, solid as rock cleft rock, rock.
riven by vein and vein, ah if it were all
so easy, to hit it & see it & feel it
buck & come clean salmon colored,
so clean I would eat it, this neat chop
takes down the spine of the world, page of
sun stripe opens, bright flesh of oak
flashes its rivers, easy to read firelight
in the new flesh, though sometimes not
so easy to break, deaf thunder of the hammer
fraction by fraction nudges the wedge in,
blow on blow not yielding at all until
28 strokes tear a jag
of shadow-lightning across the grooved
round top, black lightning slash through
the years, and the ringing of hammer and wedge
deepens from alto to baritone, rag bark falls
off and the naked grubs curl up in agony
of sunshine, or these joints the *marriage
vow* joints, what God has joined together
let no man put asunder, where the wedge not
an inch in an hour of hitting goes in and the
arms quiver exhausted, sweat soaking the crotch

of the twist shorts, and nothing, this baby
simply don't give & don't even promise just
like the nice girls back in high school, remember?,
going to be married to this flint round of
wood forever, till finally fin;al;ly it bust loose
to show the dagger-shaped knot hid in the
heart of it, black and ochre and dark red, looks like
a trawler steaming up the stream of veins,
or a stubborn island in the colorful river, what
secret part of my life is it? so resisting and
so in tight upon itself, so bitter bitter hard
until at last torn open shows that all the secret
was merely the hardness itself, there's no true
shame worth hiding but some knot of hurt
hardly recalled, yet how can I say it
is not beautiful this filigree of primaries,
its form hermetic in the flow of time the
rings transcribe, I will set it down amid
the *perfect things,* alongside the livid day
lilies here and the terrapins I brought home
as a child & kept in the cool basement
with the arrowheads and alongside Don Larsen's
Series game in 1956, for
anything so entirely itself must have value even
if it's only in the exercise of seeing it whole,
also hard are these big lengths of walnut, must
be 4 good feet across here & the wedge goes
in like a 6 penny nail & splits it no more
than a nail, have to start the other wedge here
in the little tear you couldn't mail a postcard
through, and just keep thumping away, 12-pound
sledge hefts heavy off the downswing, then bit
by bit like a political scandal it uncloses
itself except at the rugged heart the tendons
won't let go, hold on like hinges and the angle
so tight the axe head can't get in to slice clear,

have to on my knees rassle it like a hawg,
and as at last it tears I feel in my breast the
tearing, letting go reluctant as paying death
taxes, and this one piece is free though my fingers
bleed and the huge rest of the half just squats there
waiting, a whole armory of pain as dumb as stone,
but let me tell you, *Log,* godammit I already see
you stacked in the andirons blazing like a porno
starlet & as cheerfully garrulous as a general
store porch whittler, I see the life of you, yellow
red and orange and blue & hasting your dark gasses
starward, on the silverblue night splaying a new tree
shape, tree of spirit spread on the night wind,
& sifting upward to the needle pricks of
fire those bones of the heroes and monsters (Orion,
Draco, Cassiopeia, Karloff), the sweaty red
roots of this tree sizzle in our fireplace, the
ghostly arms of it embrace the moon, the lancet
glance of the star pierces its leafage, this tree
in our fireplace is the sun risen at midnight,
capillaries of heat light lift out the chimney,
the rose trellis of stars is afire, sun reaches
homeward again to the *vacant interlunar spaces,*
chimney is its shrunk trunk & pins our dwelling
to the earth and to the stars equally, this spirit
trunk in the chimney is the spine of the world,
world of darkness that huddles to the windows
& flattens its face against the panes bloodthirsty
for those entangled roots of flame and each hour
leans more heavily inward as the fire goes blue
in the rootlets & the embers heap to the shape of
a walnut meat as this grand fire begins to ponder
the problem of mortality and its arms among the
stars grow more and more tenuous, that's how it
is true the cold dark will tear our tree of fire
away complete, the hearth will cool & blacken,

the seeds of fire will blink dark one by one, but
before that and *even so* and *after all* it shall have
been a fierce glory of color, it shall have been a
goddam Hallelujah of light and warmth, warmth
enough to read by, we can read books, we can
read each others' faces, we can read the chair the
table the wall, read everything that is except the fire
itself giving us heat to read by, we can
even half read the dark that sucks the fire away
& swallows, hearth being dug out of earth &
overpowering entropy of earth clouds from the
beginning the wild root mass of fire, it was sun
jammed into dirt that raised this tree, Lucretius'
seed of fire ignis semina is seed semina mortuis
(dirt we rose from, dirt we'll never forget)
of death in that same split second, moment
split by the man's hand hard as an iron wedge
hammered into the seam between the double
eternities of zilch zip zero (& that's how man
goes forward; hits himself on the head with a hammer),
or maybe not, helluva proton here, the wood the
up quark, wedge the down quark, and man is don't
you know it buddy the *strange* q., so perhaps
the nuclear shell will hold longer than I might
have thought until until until that roaming
puddle of gravitons, a winter's night the black
hole, comes this way striding & yanks the tree
of light elongate like a sunny licorice down
the drain, yet since once I cleaned the well I'm
given to understand that here is the well that cleans
the universe and I believe it sure for the shadow
of that hardest knuckle of matter casts forward
into the flesh of light itself, see here?, this black
knar monadic and unmoving in the steady pour
of red and yellow honey of sun meat, who
knows, maybe the knot is the man or the man's

will angry against the stream of time, or is it as
they say, *the eye,* and here in the furl something
that is our unguessable double, tripledark other
punches his headbusting language through, wants
to tell us that in the antiuniverse Rimbaud is
right, that the poet encoding *can* transform all
germens with an incantatory perception of what's
what or what's supposed, the vatic will can at
the bottom trifle with an energy or two & make of
every tree that stands a *Christmas tree,* Christmas
on Earth, though even as I recall the beautiful
manifesto my faith flickers & dwindles, we are not
born for the rarer destinies only for the rarest,
we are born to enter the tree of smoke, backbone of
the world of substance, born to smear our life stuff
against the zodiac, & as I take down in matter
the spine of the world & will send it up again in
spirit a feeling that these things are so indelibly
correct overtakes me that I must pause over the half
driven wedge & water it with the sweat of my
armpit & watch my neighbor's beige terrier
ambassador of funky accidence snuffle the loud
mouthed day lilies and the tattered chips of log
and finally my sopped socks & bound away through
the fence gate as if everything round the wood
pile here were just too bleeding metaphysical
to be borne & I watch the wily jive of his
stub tail go away with something I admit like
green envy thinking why cannot my animal
wallow within himself content, why can't simply
the act of breaking the wood be plenty
enough, just the feel of it, stark augenblick
of hammer head and wedge head and then in
a while the gorgeous ripe rip of the log
broken open, sound of a watermelon dropped two
stories down, and the good ache at the bottom

of the spine and the good pain of the pocked
blister worn open the good sweat salt in my eyes,
just this and no more: the body's hungry
response to iron and wood: a primal hedonism: this
will be sufficient when I come to the wisdom
my neighbor's beige terrier possesses: but man in
his fallen state is condemned to split the tree
with his intellect all alert and doubtful, mind
fingering the restive chunks comes up empty handed,
there is I tell you in the texture of this log that
which taunts the mind & calls it simpleton and
idiot and to which the poor old browbeaten mind
acquiesces saying, All right, matter, you got me, I'm
horsewhipped & buffaloed, does that satisfy you, &
nothing happens except that matter retains its smirking
hardness & just sits there half split with how many
eons of pain stored up in the other half & says
nary a word & doesn't need to, we know what it
means or intends to mean: that when man and nature
got married they agreed never to divorce although
they knew they could never be happy & would have only
the one child Art who would bring mostly grief
to them both: but that *man always forgets* so
when here he comes with his sledge and his wedge and
an edge in his voice saying, Matter, I'm gonna
kick your ass all over this universe, matter has only
to sit quiet thinking, My man, never you heard of
passive resistance?, why that's the secret of the
world, Mexican stand off is the closest you'll get
to the heart's heat heart of the heart,
why don't you try the lotus position or the string
quartet or something equally restful, for never has
mere fever got you anywhere or me either come
to that, we could make such beautiful silence
together if only you'd slow down & shape up & let
things as they are have their guiltless pleasures,

and man replies saying unto matter, Wassamatta
you, you talking commie now all this strike talk,
I been sentenced doncha know to create reality
by the sweat of my brow, Bible sez so, take
that you hard weird pinko freak, and with this I
bring the hammer down and the wedge the old
hearthurter doesn't even *budge,* and easily it could go
on like this forever since it forever has, better take
a moment's cigarette & watch the rose petals
drop off and the day lilies scramble toward the
11 o'clock sunshine just the way this severed
tree once yearned & clutched toward, I will
sit on this log & breathe bluegray smoke (but where
shall I sit when once this flesh is spirit?) &
try to think where next to hit & smite & bash &
knock it, maybe just once on the wedge one more time,
& the wedge goes in like semen, easy as sea
current into the estuary river, & the log breaks apart
to disclose what? flesh! more flesh! flesh the
same as before and the river-clean smell of opened
flesh comes at me as the annunciation to Mary,
attar of matter, a radiance of sweet rib of wood
no man has seen before, I'm washed in the blood
of the sun, the ghostly holy of the deep deep log
interfuses me till I feel whole here and almost
cool but it doesn't come easy, I'm
here to tell you that

VI   My Grandfather's Church Goes Up

(Acts 2:1-47)
God is a fire in the head.
—Nijinsky

Holocaust, pentecost: what heaped heartbreak:

The tendrils of fire   forthrightly tasting
foundation to rooftree   flesh of that edifice . . .
Why was sear sent   to sunder those jointures,
the wheat-hued wood   wasted to heaven?
Both altar and apse   the air ascended
in sullen smoke.

                  (It was surely no sign
of God's salt grievance   but grizzled *Weird* grimly
and widely wandering.)

                  The dutiful worshipers
stood afar ghast-struck   as the green cedar shingles
burst outward like birds   disturbed in their birling.
Choir stall crushed inward   flayed planking in curlicues
back on it bending,   broad beams of chestnut
oak poplar and pine   gasht open paint-pockets.
And the organ uttered   an unholy *Omega*
as gilt pipes and pedals   pulsed into rubble.

How it all took tongue!   A total hosannah
this building burgeoned,   the black hymnals whispering
leaves lisping in agony   leaping alight,
sopranos' white scapulars   each singly singeing
robes of the baritones   roaring like rivers
the balcony bellowing   and buckling. In the basement
where the M.Y.F.   had mumbled for mercies
the cane-bottomed chairs   chirruped Chinese.
What a glare   of garish glottals

rose from the nave   what knar-mouthed natter!
And the transept tottered   intoning like tympani
as the harsh heat   held hold there.
The whole church resounded   reared its rare anthem
crying out Christ-mercy   to the cloud-cloven sky.

Those portents Saint Paul   foretold to us peoples
fresh now appeared: bifurcate fire-tongues,
and as of wild winds   a swart mighty wrestling,
blood fire and vapor   of smoke vastly vaulting,
the sun into darkness   deadened and dimmed,
wonders in heaven   signs wrought in the world:
the Spirit poured out   on souls of us sinners.
In this din as of drunkeness   the old men dreamed dreams,
the daughters and sons   supernal sights saw.
God's gaudy grace   grasped them up groaning.
Doubt parched within them   pure power overtaking
their senses. Sobbing   like sweethearts bereft
the brothers and sisters   burst into singing.
Truly the Holy   Ghost here now halted,
held sway in their hearts   healed there the hurt.

Now over the narthex   the neat little steeple
force of the fire   felt furiously.
Bruit of black smoke   borne skyward
shadowed its shutters   swam forth in swelter.
It stood as stone   for onstreaming moments
then carefully crumpled   closed inward in char.
The brass bell within it   broke loose, bountifully
pealing, plunged   plangent to the pavement
and a glamour of clangor   gored cloudward gaily.

That was the ringing that wrung   remorse out of us clean,
the elemental echo   the elect would hear always;
in peace or in peril   that peal would pull them.

Seventeen seasons   have since parted
the killing by fire   of my grandfather's kirk.

Moving of our Maker   on this middle earth
is not to be mind-gripped   by any men.

Here Susan and I   saw it, come
to this wood, wicker   basket and wool blanket
swung between us,   in sweet June
on picnic. Prattling   like parakeets
we smoothed out for our meal-place   the mild meadow grasses
and spread our sandwiches   in the sunlit greensward.
Then amorously ate.   And afterward
lay languorous and   looking lazily.
Green grass and pokeweed   gooseberry bushes
pink rambling rose   and raspberry vine
sassafrass and thistle   and serrate sawbriar
clover and columbine   clung to the remnants,
grew in that ground   once granted to God.
Blackbirds and thrushes   built blithely there
the ferret and kingsnake   fed in the footing.
The wilderness rawly   had walked over those walls
and the deep-drinking forest   driven them down.

Now silence sang: swoon of wind
ambled the oak trees   and arching aspens.

In happy half-sleep   I heard or half-heard
in the bliss of breeze   breath of my grandfather,
vaunt of his voice   advance us vaward.
No fears fretted me   and a freedom followed
this vision vouchsafed,   victory of spirit.
He in the wind   wept not, but wonderfully
spoke softly   soothing to peace.
What matter he murmured   I never remembered,
words melted in wisps   washed whitely away;
but calm came into me   and cool repose.
Where Fate had fixed   no fervor formed;
he had accepted   wholeness of his handiwork.

Again it was given   to the Grace-grain that grew it,
had gone again   gleaming to Genesis

to the stark beginning   where the first stars burned.
Touchless and tristless   Time took it anew
and changed that church-plot   to an enchanted chrisom
of leaf and flower   of lithe light and shade.

Pilgrim, the past   becomes prayer
becomes remembrance rock-real   of Resurrection
when the Willer so willeth   works his wild wonders.

VII Firewater

Beneath the hairy hams hung from the hooks
Virgil Campbell talked in his grocery store:

"I just got back from the hundredth anniversary
Of Clay County. I have kinfolks that way,
They asked me out to see the spectacle.
The local politicians—just to give you
A notion—were calling themselves *town fathers.*
So then I know something's bound to happen.
If I had fathered a town I wouldn't brag
About Hayesville. I mean, there's a matter of pride.

"First off, the usual stuff. Speeches crammed
To the gullet with lies; sorghum-judging,
Jam-judging, cake-judging, quilt-judging; ribbons
Handed out to the grandmaws and the livestock.
And then the square dance contest. (I got to say
The Hiawassee Stompers can flat out clog some . . .)
I was rolling with it right along,
Had me a laugh and a sip or two . . .   J. T.,
They had them a beauty queen. That gal was *healthy,*
I'm here to tell you, and ought to season out
As comfortable as a split rail fence
And keep as many varmints off your ground . . .
Maybe my taste is running sophisticated,
I've lived too long in the wicked city of Pigeon Fork.

"The main attraction, besides the knife- and fist-fights,
Was the Clay County Hundredth Grand Parade,
Celebrating their most famous products.
—Now what's Clay County famous for?"

                                        "Moonshine,"

My father said.
        "And everybody knows it,
But who'd've thought they'd parade it on the street?
Damn if they didn't. They went up Standing Indian
And told Big Mama to build a model still
And put it on a wagon and ride with it.
Ten years they've been trying to prosecute
That woman for running shine, and out of the blue
They come up hat in hand to ask her sweetly
To waltz it down Main Street in broad daylight.

"And she said Yes. The notion had to tickle her
Once they got past her mean suspiciousness.
So there she was. I saw her. Swear to Jesus.
Sitting in a rocking chair on a wagon
By the cooker, and the copper worm
Strung down behind her, and smoke just boiling out
Pretty as you please. A cat would've by God laughed.
Big Mama weighs close onto three hundred pounds,
But the Hayesville Beauty Queen didn't sit prouder.
She gave a special wave to the deputy sheriff.
Grinning grinning grinning like she'd stole
The courthouse weathervane. Rocking and grinning and rocking.

"Behind her came the Briar Hill Bluegrass Band
On another wagon pulled by a one-eyed mule.
That's what I thought, the way he drew to the left.
But then he'd pull the other way; and began
To kind of hop and stagger. At last he gave a lurch
And lay down in the traces and went to sleep.
Somebody hollered out, 'That mule's drunk!'
Sure enough he was. Drunk as an owl,
Just from breathing the smoke that was pouring out
From Big Mama's *model* still. The music stopped.

"Because they'd caught her at last. After all those years . . .
But what are they doing to do? They'd invited her;

They begged her to do her stuff, and so she did.
Here came the deputy. 'You're under arrest,'
He said—but smiling so the crowd would think
It was part of the act. Big Mama's boys stood up—
Wearing phony beards, barefoot with beat-up hats,
Just like the hillbillies in the funny papers—
And threw down on the deputy three shotguns.
Whether they were loaded I don't know.
He didn't know. Except Big Mama's bunch
Nobody knew. Fire don't flame as red
As that man's face. He waved them along, smiling
Till his jaw hurt. It'll take a month to relax
That smile away. They drove on around the square,
Getting their money's worth, leaving behind
That passed-out mule for the deputy to have fun with.
And went on home, back to the rocks and laurels."

"Okay," my father said, "it's good to know
The eternal verities still hold their own,
That poverty and whiskey and scratch-ankle farming
Still prop the mountains up."

                    "But it ain't that way,"
The old man said. "Big Mama's quit running corn,
Except for home use. Ain't no profit in it,
With the price of sugar up and the appetite down.
Growing these Merry Widow cigarettes,
That's where they make their money."

                          "Kind of a shame,
Tradition dying away. The funny papers
Will come to be all anybody knows."

"It ain't that bad. I know one high-grade still
Still making. If you'd care to have a snort."

"Why not?" my father said. "Time keeps grumbling on.
Let's drink us a drink: here at the end of the world."

VIII   My Father Burns Washington

Money money.
During Hoover's deep
Depression we did not have any.
Not enough to buy a night's good sleep.
My parents went to bed in the grip
Of money and dreamed of money.

We heard them walk
The resounding rooms below,
My sister and I, heard them stalk
The phantom dollar and ghostly dime. "Where to
From here?" The question always grew
Heavier in the dark.

My sister and I
Clutched hands. Money would climb
The stair, we thought, and, growling, try
The doorknob, enter upon us furiously.
Its eyes like embers in the room,
It would devour all time.

The morning brought
Chill light to lined faces.
My father spoke of other cases
Worse than ours: Miller Henson's place was
Up for sale; Al Smith had fought
And lost; Clyde Barrow got shot.

Christ, how he tried!
One job was farming, another
Teaching school, and on the side
He grubbed for Carolina Power & Light.
Came home one night to our driven mother,
Lay back his head and cried

In outrage: "Money.
Money. Money. It's the death
Of the world. If it wasn't for goddam money
A man might think a thought, might draw a breath
Of freedom. But all I can think is, Money.
Money by God is death."

Her face went hard.
"It won't always be
This way," she said. "I hear them say
It's beginning to get better." "You'd take the word
Of that political blowhard?
Old Franklin Pie-in-the-Sky?"

"Well, what's the use
Of carrying on like this?"
"It soothes my feelings." My father rose
From his chair and menaced a democratic fist
At the ceiling. "I refuse,"
He said, "to kiss their ass."

"J. T., hush!"

And now he noticed me
Shriveling in the doorway. A flush
Of shame for language spread his neck. He
Pulled me to him. A woolen crush
Of jacket rubbed my eye.

Then stood me back.
"Don't worry, hon, we'll make
Out all right . . .   But it's still true
That thinking of nothing but money makes me sick.
A man's got better things to do
Than always feeling low."

"We'll make it fine,"
She said. She tried to grin.
"I can understand how tired

You get. And I get weary to the bone.
Even so, I think—" She bit the word.
Her temper had pulled thin.

"Don't think," he said.
(That became my father's
Motto.) *"If I had my druthers:*
That's all thinking amounts to now. It withers
The will to think like that. We need
To think what *can* be had."

The argument
Seemed to die away.
He stared before him, restless silent
Despondent; we stood waiting for him to say
Whatever would ease his soul, turned flint-
Hard and moveless and dry.

He fished a green
Flimsy one dollar bill
From his pocket. "I've got it down
The philosophers are right: the root of evil
Is paper. This one at least won't kill
Another desperate man."

He got a match.
We listened, frozen in time,
To the ugly inarticulate scratch
And watched the tender blooming of the flame.
"I never figured on getting rich."
Revenge was sweet with doom.

He lit the single.
When the corner caught
We felt a minatory tingle
Advance our skins. Had he truly taught
Us freedom, amid our paralyzed mangle
Of motive and black thought?

It made no more
Lovely a fire than any
Other fuel: a flame and a char
Of paper. We couldn't think of it as money
Burning but as oxidized despair
Climbing the indifferent air.

He wept as it burned,
Then flung it down and ground
The corner out and, ashen, turned
To face my mother who smiled and frowned
At once. Like a beaten child he mourned:
"Mother, will it still spend?"

IX   Burning the Frankenstein Monster:
Elegiac Letter to Richard Dillard

It is Henry, as everyone knows, who's really the monster,
   Not the innocent wistful crazy-quilt of dead flesh
We remember as being in love with flowers and children like flowers.
   It's the will made totally single which frightens us,
Monstrum horrendum, informe, ingens, cui lumen ademptum:
   Virgil's misshapen eyeless one-eye gone mad
And disturbing the fabric of ongoing time. —You were right, Richard,
   What I mostly ripped off from Rimbaud was the notion of fire
   As symbolic of tortured, transcendent-striving will.

(But *The Inkling* is long out of print, bemuses not even my mother.
   Let it smolder to ash on whatever forgotten shelf.)

Why must poor Karloff be born out of fire, and die, fire-fearing,
   In the fire? Is he truly our dream of Promethean man?
Does he warn us of terrible births from atomic furnaces, atomic
   Centuries, shambling in pain from the rose-scented past?
Having been burned and then drowned, reversing the fate of Shelley,
   The lame monster brings back upon us the inverted weight
Of the romantic period. Whose children we are, but disinherit,
   Stranded in decades when all is flame and nothing but flame.

And my vividest memory: light first seen by the monster, pouring
   Through the roof peeled back little by little, at last
Bathing in splendor the seamed unlovable face with its stricken
   Eyes; and the creature in agony uplifting his hands,
Whimpering gutturally, hoping to be drawn up like water vapor
   Into the full forgiving embrace of the progenitor Sun.
What wouldn't *we* give to undergo in our latter years the virgin
   Onslaught of light? To be born again into light,
To be raised from the grave, rudimentary senses unfolding like flowers
   In a warm April rainfall . . .   But then they reseal the roof;

Little by little his hands drop again to his sides and the brightness
    Lapses in stone-colored eyes, his mind huddles forlorn.

Henry is watching in barely controlled hysteria, thinking
    Thoughts inarticulate, biting his rag-like hands.
He is a child of the lightning also, of the flash unrepeated
    Revelation which blasts and creates in an instant, all.
Flash he must follow to destruction, before us melting whitely
    To madness. Let him then marry, let the wine be fetched
Out of the family cellars, the servants giggling like tipsy chickens
    When the baron proposes his toast: "A son to the House
Of Frankenstein!" —Has he forgotten that Henry already has fathered
    A son given over to the care of Fritz, dark spirit of Earth?

Fritz is unbearable. Crazy perhaps and certainly turned evil
    By reason of fear, it's he who teaches the monster to fear,
Perverting the light to a means of torture. This troll always scurrying
    Upstairs and down with a torch in his hand is reduced
Finally to shadow, to shadow hanged and splayed on the prison
    Wall. This is justice, of course, but it horrifies the mad
Doctor, the sane doctor, and every one of those whose consciences
    Whisper: *The fault is yours, for the dead must bury the dead.*

Return to the lake where the two abandoned children are playing:
    Here is no murder, no trial of death upon life.
Entrancement of naked simplicity washes both the bright faces;
    Pastoral daisies, the currency of joy between two,
Float in the water; the monster is struggling to utter first laughter.
    Now the sweet daisies are gone, and the hands that had held them ache,
Tremble with joylessness. Suddenly metaphor is born to the injured
    Criminal brain, and he plucks a final white bloom,
Launches it silvery drifting. The death of all flowers forever
    Is accomplished. From moist green ground he has plucked his own death.

Nuptials broken . . . The father in silent dry-eyed accusation
    Brings to the wedding the single drowned flower of death . . .
(Notice in horror films, Richard, how weddings impendent on science,
    Knowledge unborn, recur. In *Dracula, Curse*

Of the Demon, in Freund's *The Mummy,* in Hillyer's *Dracula's*
    Daughter, in *Dr. Jekyll and Mr. Hyde.*
Hearing "the loud bassoon," but prevented—until we listen
    To Salvation's full passion—the church, we stand aghast.
Faith calls to faith, but our faith must be earned from terror, consummate
    Love must be thirsted for, light must be wholly desired.)

White-gowned Elizabeth sees in the mirror the wayward monster
    (Calendar girl who confronts a medieval death's-head);
Hears the low growl, a deep rasp as if earth were tearing in tatters;
    Obligingly faints. And the monster her bridegroom lifts
Her over the threshold, through door after door, but the ritual is empty.
    Only one union is Karloff permitted: to wed
Terribly the flames, to return to the trauma of being fathered
    Once again, conceived in the raging delirium of fire.

    Father and son, they are bound to a wheel of crazed fire.

Father and son, with one instant of recognition between them:
    Jagged and hungry the gears that ponderously chew
The circle, and father and son for a moment pause to examine.
    "You who brought me into this world what have you done?"
"No. Never you I sired but a healthy longed-for imago."
    "I am but I and I come now to claim my birthright."
"Born of my will from the grave, for you this world holds nothing."
    "Maker and monster we shall not die apart."

Richard, this world is ever the world the fathers fashioned.
    Right and the right to be right belong to dreams
Not as yet come into flesh. The courageous monsters perish
    Always alone, and yet always in a final light
Glorious and stark. As the hilltop mill is always burning,
    Raising its arms of clean blaze against the stars.

X   Bloodfire

(Of the fire-martyrs of the war: the immolated and self-immolated)

Siblings scorch-eyed and aloof
Now you lie across the wars
Emblazoning a worst reproof
Of promises broken, burning scars
Of an inhuman politic.
Now floods into the plundered heart
Sick pity for the querulous sick,
The garrulous dead. No more apart
You lie entwined in rank blood.

I recognized you from the first.
Struggling in your sweat-soaked bed
You wept, your head ablaze with thirst
For absolution. Where was none.
The bitter uproot shouting throng
You saw frustrate upon your screen,
But knew you never could belong
To another army, however right
In motive, cause, and claim, however
Righteous it appeared on sight.
Yours was the holy importunate fever.

Now to my door the papers bring
Your names or the names of towns that die.
New promises flourish now; late spring
has brought the Pentagon's newest lie.
But nothing's new. The same machine
Toils on, grinding out the stats.
Westmoreland's photogenic grin
Assures: more gold braid on more hats.

In every politician's tattle,
Bloat exigencies of shame,

34

You heard within his words the rattle
Of M-14s, the skin-tight flame
Of phosphorous grenades, strafing
Of paddies, unmanned hospitals leveled,
Children murdered past believing.
In sleepless fear of God you groveled.

And rose to mornings of fresher lies,
Of newspapers smeared with the greasy smirk
Of a thief whose principles green flies
Wouldn't shit on in his hatefilled dark.
Your heart fell ill at the sun coming up.
Coffee gagged you. You rode to work
Past faces that had lost their grip,
Each feature a featureless mark.

Trembling I read the same accounts.
I too suffered, I was there.
I watched them kill for brownie points.
My sleep too dissolved in fire.

Terror engorged us. Television,
Little gray cage with its black joke,
Brought us our latest Sense of Mission
And the new installment of *Gunsmoke*.
That was *our* light at the end of the tunnel.
And in our TV dinners we found
Hands and eyeballs in a neat little bundle.
Who among us was not stoned?

Here I stopped. Here I turned
Back to the books that nurtured me
When I met evil first, learned
An implacable philosophy.
But you went on. Striving striving
In the lightless void to know
What best to make of guilty living
In a decade without love or law.

When everything had gone so far
The center was past the edge, you fell
To pieces, let their dirty war
Possess you. You invited hell;
Decided not another dawn
Would see you powerless to say
The sentence someone had to say:
We now divorce this filthy game.
Then in the bluest hour of day
You died, and rose again in flame.

And still we die.
And rise in flame.

XI   Bloodfire Garden

It is the disease
necessary to know God.
It is the heat
in the animal calling to animals,
        Take me into your world of blade and rock
help me return   to when the sun
first struck off in fury
the boiling planets.

It is the fever reaching down
to the fluid core of earth,
connection
with first daybreak lapping
the unstarred walls of time,
connection
with beginning.
                It is
desire.
It is the skin
sniffing the skin of the other,
and convulsion of heart's-blood
when the woman turns from watching
through the window, unloosens
the halter-strings,
steps forward gravely, and on
the bedside table
sows a handful of bobby pins.

It is the flame which obsesses silence.

        Love, in the fire we are
whole again,

our atoms driven and
interlocked as heat in air;
after the slow blind tracings
we leap up scarlet in fire,
star-shudder overcomes our limbs when we strain
one another against fire-mesh,
straining our figures elongate,
toe-tip to fingertip,
like candleflames in the new wind
sprung at twilight.

     This is the gleam
I starved after when
at twelve years I saw
in some nestle on the mountains at midnight
the hunters' campfire
blinking blinking
and walked in the dark to the edge
of the river,
and could go no farther,
but looked there upon
Orion
sliding the water calmly.

Now you warm me.

The snap.
It is the snap I remember
in the fresh-turned late-March garden.
  My father by the chicken
wire fence scythed short
the blackberry vine,
scribble scribble scribble
raked up in barbarous heaps,
his flint hands
steady in solid arcs across.
We put it to torch.

Clean clear
flame against mauve sunset.

Now I have come to do
the thing my father has done.

Earthsmoke
mauve in late mauve light.

The snap:
it is the sound
of shackles broken,
ice-fracture under the weight
of the mountain, clap of cut glass
coming apart, the far-off
report of oak break.
. . . Writhed in white fire.
Thorn-points firing,
sizzle on the hard
vine ribs purple green
oiled and red-streaked
frying lattice
of dry bones.

I prayed then by the thorn fire.

I went stark sane, feeling under my feet
the hands of blackberry fire
rummaging
unfurrowed earth.
At that hour in shadowy
garden ground
the ghosts began again to take flesh.

(And in the west murky corner the poison
wild cherry we girdled
to kill.)

      Love, after the snap
and the deep shudder

a cool invisible smoke goes up
from our bodies, it is grateful
prayer, sigil
of warm silence between us.

In this garden our bed we have burned
down again to the ghost of us,
green Aprils collide
in our blood.

Burnt-off, we are being prepared.
The seeds of fresh rain advance,
wind bearing from the south,
out of the green isles
of Eden.